John L. Wellington

The Gold Fields of Alaska

How to Reach and Operate them

John L. Wellington

The Gold Fields of Alaska
How to Reach and Operate them

ISBN/EAN: 9783337715830

Printed in Europe, USA, Canada, Australia, Japan

Cover: Foto ©Andreas Hilbeck / pixelio.de

More available books at **www.hansebooks.com**

THE GOLD FIELDS OF

❧ ALASKA ❧

HOW TO REACH AND OPERATE THEM.

BY JOHN L. WELLINGTON

A thrilling account of Mr. Wellington's successful trip into that country during the past season. In which he gives all the maps, statistics and such other general advice and information of interest to prospecting parties.

———

PUBLISHED AND FOR SALE BY

THE BUCKNER PRINTING CO.

CRIPPLE CREEK, COLO.

PUBLISHER'S NOTICE.

—o—

After going through the regular account of his own experience in Alaska, Mr. Wellington has prepared an Appendix in the back of the book, containing much general information and advice for the special benefit of parties desiring to enter the gold fields.

This will be of great assistance to inexperienced parties in giving them an idea of the best sections of the country to visit, and in helping them to select their provisions and equipments for this long hazardous journey with care and judgement.   No one expecting to undertake the trials and hardships of the trip should fail to read this account and take a copy of it with him, as it contains much practical information that can not be obtained elsewhere, and the most complete and reliable maps that are to be had.

INTRODUCTORY

The gold fields of Alaska are fast becoming the gieatest placer mining district in the world. The estimated output for 1896 is $6,000,000. Outside of the enormous business that the stamp mills are doing on the southern cost, there are about 300 miners in the Yukon district alone who average $20 a day working their own ground, and many more who have been fortunate in locating claims whose daily output is vastly greater.

The regular wages paid for placer mining are $10 per day, and such is the richness of the district, that ground that will not yield as much as $20 daily per man is not considered worth working and is left lying idle.

Gold is found scattered widely along the river beds, almost throughout the entire extent of Alaska, in paying quantities, but the mad rush of miners is for the richest districts that have already been discovered, where a fortune may be made in a season.

This is a vast country with a wonderful future before it. There are thousands of miles of river beds that have never been explored, offering room and opportunity for all who care to endure the hardships for the sake of becoming rich.

Even outside of its gold fields, Alaska is one of the most interesting countries on the globe. It is called the land of the midnight sun, where they have night all winter and day all summer. Its rivers and glaciers are wonders in themselves, and in no part of the globe is better fishing and hunting to be found. The interior abounds in big game, the rivers are alive with geese and ducks, and along the coast, walrus, seal and polar bear are pentiful enough.

During the long winter, storms are frequent and the country is rapidly covered with snow and ice. It is a common trick of the Thermometer to fall 60 or 80 degrees below zero, and when it is remembered that the trip into the interior must be made by sled over a barren, frozen country for seven or eight hundred miles, something of the hardships to be endured can be imagined.

The start is ordinarily made in the latter part of march from Juneau City, where supplies are to be purchased and an outfit carefully equipped. The course from there is generally over a snowy chain of mountains that skirts the southern coast of Alaska, by way of Chilkoot pass, where you are likely to be frozen to death if you lack the patience to wait for good weather before attempting to cross this giant mountain of ice.

After successfully crossing this dreaded pass you will find yourself confronted by Miles' Canon, White Horse Rapids and Five Fingers that stand like giant sentinels in the river to dispute your further progress into the country. If you are successful in passing through these dangerous places, then your trials for the time being are over and you will have a pleasant sail down the mighty Yukon river into the greatest placer gold district on earth.

It was early in the spring of 1896 that I started out with two companions from San Francisco to try my fortune in this Eldorado of the north. What befell us on this journey, our rather remarkable trials, misfortunes and successes, I have set forth in the following chapters, to which I invite your further inspection.

J. L. W.

THE GOLD FIELDS OF

❧ ALASKA ❧

HOW TO REACH AND OPERATE THEM.

CHAPTER I.

The great gold valley of the Yukon is reached by two routes. One of these is by steamer up the Yukon river, a distance of 5,000 miles from San Francisco. This is a long and expensive journey, putting you into the mining district rather late in the season.

Very few miners take that course; most seem to prefer the shorter though more hazerdous route by way of Juneau City, thence over the dreaded Chilkoot pass by sled and down a chain of lakes and tributaries by boat to the mighty Yukon.

After spending a week in San Francisco, making some necessary purchases for the journey, our little party of three bought tickets and took passage on one of the Pacific Coast Steamship Co's vessels bound for Juneau. A number of steamers belonging to this Company ply up and down the coast, making regular trips northward weekly and cut-rate excursions all through the summer to Alaska. These excursions are themselves very pleasent trips, even if one has no particular desire to visit this wonder-land of the north.

The rates quoted for 1896 for first class passage from San Francisco to Juneau City are $18 to $25, and about one-half that amount for second class.

On these steamers each individual is allowed to take 150 pounds free of charge.

After getting our baggage properly stowed away, we had not long to wait before we heard the welcome cry of "Ready—All aboard"—and off we go! The steamer carefully wound its way out among the multitude of vessels anchored about the docks, and it was not long before we were considerably out to sea. Then we bid farewell to this smoking mart of the Pacific and were soon fairly started on our long journey north.

It is about 1600 miles from San Francisco to the little city Juneau set snugly in against a mountain peak on the southern coast of Alaska. Though rather early in the spring, we found the weather pleasant enough and the trip very enjoyable.

Skirting along at no great distance from the coast, we had occasion to see some very pretty scenery shoreward, while thousands of interesting islands from time to time put in their appearance about us, some very small and others empires in themselves.

As we approached Alaska, we found the
northward view obstructed, for hundreds of
miles along the southern coast, by a range
of snowy peaked mountains that must be
crossed before the great valley of the Yukon
is reached, where such a mad rush of gold
seekers has been going on for the past few
years.

Scattered along this southern coast are
several ports of some importance, including
Juneau, the mining and money center of the
district, and Sitka its sleepy old capital.

Our vessel had occasion to stop at several of these places before we reached Juneau. On arriving at that quiet little city,
we found much that was of interest to us
during our short stay there. The place is
well supplied with hotels, restaurants, general business stores, &c., that are reasonable
enough in price considering their distance
from the commercial world.

This is the outfitting point for most parties going over the range to the gold fields. Special outfitting stores here will supply you with all the necessary provisions and equipments for making the journey inland.

It is sometimes the method of inexperienced parties to leave the selection and putting up of this outfit to the merchant from whom it is purchased, but it seems to me that any one not having confidence enough in his own judgement to select and pack an outfit even for a hazerdous journey like this, would be lacking in the necessary ingenuity and strength of character to successfully battle with the trials and hardships of the interior where there is a possibility of starvation or freezing to death.

It became necessary now for us to complete our equipments and make preparations for departing. This we did immediately, by purchasing a sufficient supply of flour, beans, bacon, sugar, coffee, &c., to last us for eight months. We also took with us, besides plenty of clothing and light warm bedding, two Yukon sleighs, a light windlass and a good quantity of rope, a tent, a folding sheet iron stove and cooking vessels, and a good supply of nails, hammers, axes, picks, shovels and many other miscellaneous articles.

It will be remembered that we had previously made some necessary purchases in San Francisco for the journey. These consisted of fur clothing, rubber boots and coats, arms, amunition, &c., any of which may be purchased in Juneau at slightly advanced prices.

Before starting, we had also constructed a boat of galvanized-iron for use on the lakes and rivers. This we afterward found to be of great service, for it was light and easily portable where it would have been very difficult to take anything like a heavy wooden boat. It was 18 feet long, 4 feet broad at the top, 30 inches at the bottom, and had a depth of 2½ feet. It was strongly built of extra heavy galvanized iron, being ribbed and braced in such a manner as to make it thorroughly substantial.

This boat weighed 200 pounds and would safely carry more than a ton. One feature about it that made it of great convenience was the fact of its being built in three different sections, water tight and independent of one another so far as floating qualities were concerned. Its middle section was 6½ feet long and its front and rear sections each a little less in length, thus making it convenient to pack the sections inside of one another when it became necessary to ship it.

The sections weighed about 65 pounds each, thus making it easily portable around canons and dangerous places in the rivers;

and for ordinary heavy usage the three sections could be quickly and substantially bolted together. For light rowing and hunting purposes the middle section could be left in camp and the front and rear sections bolted together, thus forming a neat and convenient little boat.

It must be remembered that each section was water-tight in itself, and if one section should be snagged, which was rarely the case, the other two, being dry, would be sufficient to keep the boat afloat until repairs could be made. But this was a trouble that seldom delayed us, for the front section, being most exposed, was made of extra heavy iron doubled.

CHAPTER II

From Juneau there are four different routes leading into the interior, through as many different passes of the coast range. That usually taken is through a gap in the mountains known as Chilkoot Pass.

The summit of this pass is 115 miles north of Juneau, and the first hundred miles of this distance is covered by steamer.

In the latter part of March we got our supplies together and took passage on a little craft going to Dyea Inlet about 100 miles north of Juneau This is the head of salt water and usual landing place of parties taking this route.

The fare is $10 and the trip is ordinarily made in 12 hours when the weather is good; but before rounding the lower end of Duglas Island such terrific waters were encountered from the Takou river that we were delayed many hours. A cutting north wind was sweeping down the valley of the Takou, and like an angered demon it came roaring out from the river's mouth, lashing the foaming water into mountainous billows, and in its rage tossing volumes of spray high over the top of Grand Island.

Up to this point all had been easy going with our little party, but now for the first time, the continued surging of the waters and the terrific bellowing of the north wind, sweeping down like a hurricane from the arctic reigons, reminded us of the many hardships to be endured before we would be able to cross the interior and reach comfortable shelter and companionship.

After a prolonged struggle of several hours, during which our little craft was all but foundered, we succeeded in steaming around the head of Duglas Island and proceeded safely up the Dyea river. There on a sandbank some 15 miles from the renouned Chilkoot Pass, the boat landed us, bid us a farewell and left our little party to battle with the elements as best it knew how.

It might be well to state here that my two companions were brothers, Jim and John T. McCormic. Both of them were experienced miners, one from the Cripple Creek district and the other, whom we picked up in California, an old timer in the placer fields of that state.

It was an advantage for me to make the trip with these gentlemen. From long acquaintanceship I knew them to be reliable and trustworthy, besides being remarkably persevering and absolutely fearless. I would not care to make this hazerdous trip into Alaska with any one who has not the stability and will power to calmly stare Death in the face and if need be laugh him out of countenance.

Turning again to the account in hand, we see a long stretch of tide-swept sand extending along the water's edge and forming the only visible land about us, for snow was everywhere in abundance.

Jumbled together upon the bank, our equipments did not form a very interesting prospect as compared with the glittering scenery about us and beyond us in the mountains. But we did not allow ourselves to be delayed long in the contemplation of this beautiful scenery, for the north wind kept up an unpleasant moaning about us and the rapid rising of the tide warned us that we had not any too much time to gather up our chattels and get off the possessions of the Ocean.

All of our perishable goods in the way of provisions and supplies were put up in strong water-tight bags averaging about 50 pounds each, thus making them easy to handle and precluding any possibility of their becoming damaged by water.

After substantially bolting the sections of our boat together and mounting it on the two sleds. we loaded in our supplies and made immediate preparations for departing. Our route lay up the valley of the Dyea river. a small stream rising near the foot of Chilkoot Pass. After getting our sleighs on the frozen surface of this stream, we found it easy enough going for a while; but as we advanced the snow grew deeper rapidly and before we had covered the distance of five miles from our starting point, we found it very difficult to get along at all.

After struggling through a two foot snow all the afternoon, we succeeded in reaching the forks of the river about seven miles from our starting point, and being completely exhausted, we camped here for the night. Without making any attempt to put up our tent, we gathered around the boat and partook of a hearty meal.

Under such circumstances a bed is ordinarily made for the night by spreading hemlock brush a foot deep on the snow and covering it with canvas and blankets; but our boat contained three departments sufficiently long to make comfortable sleeping quarters, and we found it easy enough to stretch a stout canvas over their full length and support it by means of props in the boat. This formed as comfortable sleeping quarters as one could wish and we retired for the night.

The wind had laid and the silence about us was intense, broken only by the frequent call of geese flying northward and the soft pelting of heavy snow drops on the canvas stretched above us. It was snowing and as harmlessly as it seemed to fall about us, we knew that it boded ill for us on the morrow. We were not mistaken, for at daylight we awoke and found ourselves completely engulfed in a five foot snow.

After breakfasting we broke our way along slowly through this soft impediment, stopping every few hundred yards to rest. But at last our progress became so slow and tiresome that we had to resort to the practice known as "doubling". Unloading our boat we left about one-half of the weight behind, taking forward with us one sled and the middle section of the boat loaded.

The first half of the day was spent in breaking our way through the snow to a place known as Sheep Camp only five miles from the forks of the river. Here we de_ cided to camp for the night, and after taking a short rest, we returned at once for our other goods. It was easy enough to bring up this last section for the trail was already broken, and we succeeded in getting back to Sheep Camp long before night.

We were now about twelve miles from the coast that we had left the day previous, and had something like three miles yet to cover before reaching the summit of the pass. This camp was at the upper limit of timber and practically at the foot of the pass.

A scattering growth of stunted spruce-trees stretched away far below us to the ocean, and great precipitous slopes of snow and ice towered above us looking not a little discouraging. Through a long gorge enclosed by the steep walls of snow-covered mountains, we could see at the summit, thousands of feet above, a little gap known as the Chilkoot Pass, the gateway to the Yukon valley.

The seriousness of the task before us was now apparent. Taking about one-third of our suppliet we pressed forward with a will and succeeded in re· ching the foot of the last and hardest part or the ascent, about a half-mile from the summit. Here we decided to stop for the night and hurried back at once to bring up the rest of our supplies. We found the ascent easier than we expected, for the snow at this altitude was frozen just hard enough to afford good footing.

From this camp it is about one-half mile to the summit, but the route is through a deep trough of glittering ice and hard-crusted snow as steep as the roof of a house, with huge masses of precipitous mountains on either hand burried in perpetual snow and ice, nobody knows how deep.

After passing a remarkably stormy night in which the wind howled about us drifting a torrent of sleet and snow down the gorge, we were up at daylight to find the sky clear and the air sharp as a knife's edge.

Taking a portion of our supplies on one of the sleds, we started out boldly to make the last and most difficult part of the ascent, zigzagging our way slowly along up this glistening trough of ice. But we had not proceeded far before the ascent became so steep and slippery that we had to resort to the common method of cutting every foot-step in the ice with a hatchet. This was painfully slow work and it was something like three hours before we were able to cover the short distance and rest upon the narrow crest of frozen snow and ice that divides the great Yukon basin from the mighty ocean.

CHAPTER III

It was almost dark before we got everything to the top of the pass and sat down on our sleds to look back over the dizzy trail of snow and ice stretching away thousands of feet below us to the ocean.

The course is only fifteen miles in length, but it had taken us three days of excessive labor to traverse it, and with a sigh of relief we turned our backs upon it and bid farewell to hotels, restaurants, stores, and all the conventional forms and laws of society and civilization as they are the outgrowth of organized governments.

Jumbled about us on either hand were great masses of craggy peaks burried forever in a perpetual sheet of snow and ice, glittering in the last rays of the setting sun; but our gaze was fixed more intently to the northward, where the great valley of the Yukon and its gold-freighted tributaries stretches away in spotless billows of white, with neither rock, nor tree, nor shrub, nor any visible signs of life to mar the beauty of that vast blanket of snow rolling away to the northward as far as the eye could see.

After passing a disagreeable night on the summit, we tied everything on the sleds in the morning and started down the steep decent at a lively pace. The snow was frozen hard and we found it difficult to controle the sleds, so we decided to get on board and turn them loose, taking chances with whatever obstructions we might encounter in a wild ride down the broad bottom of the gorge.

The lseds were heavy laden and with our extra weight added to them they flew down the glassy slope with the speed of an express train, writhing and screaking under the weight and sometimes clearing the snow for thirty feet at a bound.

No sooner had we got well under headway than we began to wonder how we were to stop, and we were not long in finding out.

As we flew down the broad bottom of the gorge at a dangerously increasing speed, bounding over one eminence after another, we overtook and passed an Indian scudding along on snowshoes. At this point we noticed that the snow was becoming softer in the descent, and about a half mile below our front sleigh swung around to the left over some obstruction, and dashing off down a small ravine, jumped a steep embankment and tumbled us pell-mell into a deep drift of soft snow at the bottom.

For a few moments the air was full of flying snow, tin cans, blankets, saws, provisions and a sinful waste of profanity. By the time we had scrambled up a little and began to realize our situation, the Indian had overtaken us and was standing on the precipice above peering down at our pitiable condition with something like a grin on his sallow sunken face. He took in the situation at a glance, and without a word began to fish after us with a long pole he carried with him having an iron hook attached to the end of it.

We were in the pit, and I might say in the soup, and the form working above us with the hook bore such a striking resemblance to that usually ascribed to the evil one, that we were afterwards led to name this worthy fellow Mephisto.

It is now only a short distance to the head of Lake Linderman, where a little stream bubbling up from the ground creeps away under the snow forming the very beginning of the mighty Yukon river. This is the first of a series of lakes, from three to thirty miles in length, that form the upper Yukon. These lakes remain frozen until June and must be crossed by means of sleighs, requiring many a long hard day's portage. Ordinarily a strong wind is blowing from the south, and by erecting a large canvas sail, we were able to scud along over the surface of most of them with comparative ease.

The last two lakes of the chain, Lake Marsh and Lake Lebarge, are connected by a river fifty-five miles in length, but in this short space are the greatest obstructions to river navigation in the whole Yukon system.—Miles Canon and the White Horse Rapids. Miles Canon, above everything else is dreaded by Yukon travellers. More than a dozen men have gone down with their boats in this wild maelstrom of water never to rise again.

Above the canon, the river is about three hundred feet wide. At its mouth it suddenly contracts to thirty feet, and increasing its velocity to twenty miles an hour rushes with maddening force through a c anon with absolutely perpendicular walls a hundred feet high and three-quarters of a mile long.

After successfully crossing Lake Marsh we found the river open, and packing everything in the boat, we floated down the stream. The Indian who had helped us out of the pit was practically without provisions or any visible means of support outside of a very fine Winchester with which he was remarkably skillful. After taking a long strong pull at a flask we had with us, he very readily consented to accompany our party under the condition that he be allowed to indulge in this same pull occasionally. He had traversed the course we were following several times, and being well posted on many subjects connected with the country, he proved a valuable addition to our party.

On reaching the mouth of Miles Canon, we found a landing and looked about us a little. Truly it was a formidable looking place, with a thundering torrent of water rushing madly through a long narrow gap in the rock. Mephisto said it would take us about four days to carry our supplies around it and two minutes to run boldly through. He stated further that he had run through twice with other parties and expressed a willingness to take the boat through by himself under condition that he be allowed an immediate draw at the flask; but this was not our way of doing business. We gave him a dram, however, and stationed him in front to do the steering, as he knew the course best. Then we all got in and let her go. Down she went like a rocket, swaying with the current and churning up and down like a bucking bronco. By frantic paddling, we managed to keep her in the middle of the stream and off from the walls against which so many boats have been smashed like an egg-shell. So deafening is the roar of the waters and so quick and exciting the run, that I doubt whether anybody in the boat, outside of Mephisto, realized what was taking place, until it was all over and all danger passed.

Below the canon the river spreads out to its normal width in a series of rapids that culminate three miles below in the White Horse, a bad piece of water that we found it necessary to carry our supplies around, going into camp at the foot of the rapids.

From this camp it was about twenty-five miles down the river to Lake Lebarge, the last and largest of the chain. On reaching this lake, we found it still frozen, but the ice was so soft that it was very difficult to get our sleighs along. After dragging our supplies along through the sloppy ice for three long days, we reached the lower end of the lake and again found open water. From the excessive labor, we were worn out, wet and bedraggled: and the elder

McCormic made Mephisto a present of a pint bottle of liquor for the valuable services he had rendered us during this long portage.

I never saw an Indian so elated in my life, and from this forward, I believe he would have stuck his head into a flaming furnace for our sake. His first impulse was to lick the bottle dry and fairly chew the cork into small bits ;then in course of half an hour, he was becoming pretty well intoxicated, and began to be very communicative. He sat down on a log and told us a long story of a series of rich gold bars he had found far up on a tributary of the Yukon. After finishing his story, he asked for another dram of whiskey, and McCormic gave it to him. Then he invited us to go and help him work his claims, offering us an equal share in the rich deposits along the stream. In the meanwhile he was fumbling about his clothing, seemingly with an effort to find something. He said that he had some

fine gold-specimens about him somewhere
that he had taken out the previous season,
but that he would be unable to find them
unless he had another drink to quiet his
nerves.   Things were becoming interesting and McCormic gave him another dram,
whereupon he produced a greasy deerskin
pouch and poured out into his cap about
three ounces of the finest gold nuggets I
have ever seen.

CHAPTER IV.

In the morning after Mephisto had recovered from his intoxication he went over the story of his gold claims again and insisted that we should go and help him work them. He said that he had washed out $2,000 by himself during the last season, and with a knowing jesture at the liquor jug he indicated where it had all gone to.

After carefully considering the matter, we decided that we had nothing to loose and all to gain, as the vacinity into which he wanted to take us would at least afford interesting prospecting; so the boat was launched again with Mephisto as a delighted guide and we dropped down the stream to the junction of Pelly River. We afterwards passed White River on our left and Stewart on our right, and then for six long weeks, day after day, we pulled against strong currents and contrary winds, carrying our supplies around many falls and rapids, until we had begun to think that our red friend would never call a halt.

We were now in one of the wildest and most heavy wooded countries I have ever seen, and one day when we were far up near the head of a little creek, Mephisto announced the fact that our journey was at an end, and we went into camp under the lee of a great bluff, with pine trees towering everywhere about us and a fine spring bubbling from the ground.

After prospecting the stream sufficiently to learn the richness of the district, all washing was abandoned and we went to work with a will to felling trees and sawing up lumber for the purpose of constructing sluice boxes.

The spring was now well advanced and the sun began to circle about the heavens, never going out of sight, and before long all the mountains and the valleys were covered with the most luxuriant growth of flowers imaginable. A great variety of game was in abundance everywhere, even in the immediate vicinity of our camp, and Mephisto kept us supplied with the choicest of fresh meets.

After getting our sluice boxes in operation, we kept a continual stream of dirt and gravel washing through them all the time, and such was the richness of the bars, that we were able to clear up from $400 to $1000 per day. The season was well advanced and we knew that within a couple of months the north wind would be sweeping down on us with a torrent of sleet and snow, freezing the ground and making further progress very difficult. So we worked with a will all the time, hardly taking time to eat and sleep, and at the end of sixty days, we had succeeded in taking out $48,000 worth of very fine nuggets.

After closing operations for the season, we looked the ground over carefully and came to the conclusion that we had hardly made any impression on the deposits of this rich district. We made an estimate that there were more than a million dollars worth of gold imbeded in the bars of this little creek.

The summer was now far advanced, and the indications were for cold weather soon. As we wanted to reach the Yukon and get out before the river froze, we thought it a good plan to start at once for the course down stream was a long and difficult route.

Mephisto expresssed a desire to stay in camp during the winter, as he wanted to do some trapping and considered the locality very promising for that purpose. So we left many of our equipments with him and what provisions we had except enough to last us until we reached Forty Mile. As it is our intention to work the claims during the coming season, Mephisto agreed to come overland on his snowshoes to Circle City early in tne spring and help us bring up supplies to last through the next summer. We left him in the operation of building a kind of hut for winter quarters, and in all probability he will be able to gather in as much as $2000 worth of furs during the winter.

Taking the boat and a few supplies, we started on our long journey down stream, passing successfully through Forty Mile c mp and reaching Circle City several days before the last steamer of the season started down the river homeward bound.

The McCormic brothers decided to spend the winter in Circle City, so I took passage on the steamer by myself and made the long trip down the Yukon river and back on the Pacific Ocean to San Francisco.

APPENDIX.

GENERAL NOTES OF INTEREST.

WAGES

$1000 is the amount of a seasons wages in the Yukon district.

Circle City has doubled in population this summer and anyone who can handle a saw and hammer has no difficulty in securing employment.

A Chilkat Indian arrived in Juneau last week from Circle City with $1600 in gold dust, the result of a year's labor about the trading posts of the Yukon.

$10 per day are the regular wages paid to miners, but men have been offered $12 per day in Circle City to go to the new diggings along the various creeks, and men who do not care to work claims of their own will find little difficulty in securing employment.

TRANSPORTATION.

About thirty horses have been taken to Circle City during the past summer for transportation purposes. The trip inland, usually made by dogs, sleighs and boat, has been very successfully covered lately by means of horses across the country. Grass abounds everywhere and an abundance of hay can be cut and cured to last stock through the winter.

It is a difficult matter to get supplies from Circle City and Forty Mile to the various camps situated along the small creeks of the district, as much as sixty and eighty cents per pound being charged for their transportation.

In the winter dogs and sleighs are employed for this purpose, but during the hot summer months what can not be packed on the backs of dogs must be carried by human agency. But the taking in of a drove of cattle and a number of horses during the season will grately facilitate the matter of transportation.

MISCELLANEOUS NOTES.

Forty Mile is just in side the British possessions.

Circle City is 200 miles down the river.

Harper's trading post is at the mouth of Pelly river.

Dalton's trading post is on the head waters of the Alsec river.

Only 300 feet can be taken up in a claim by one man.

$5 per foot per year is the tax levied on claims in the British possessions.

No tax is charged on claims in American possessions.

There are 25 mounted police at Forty Mile.

There is no law at Circle City but miners' law.

Forty Mile creek, Birch creek, Mastodon creek, Eagle creek, Deadwood creek, Bonanza creek, and Harrison Creek are a few of the small streams that are being worked and are found to be wonderfully rich in gold deposits.

TABLE OF DISTANCES.

FROM JUNEAU

		MILES.
To	Haines (Chilkat)	80
"	Dyea (Chilkoot)	100
"	Head of canoe navigation	106
"	Summit of Chilkoot Pass	115
"	Lake Linderman (length 6 mi)	124
"	Lake Bennett (length 26 mi)	129
"	Lake Takou	175
"	Takish House	179
"	Mud Lake	180
"	Lake Marsh (length 23 mi)	200
"	Miles Canon	225
"	White Horse Rapids	228
"	Boundary bet. B. C. & N. W. T.	139
"	Takheena River	240
"	Lake LeBarge (length 32 mi)	256
"	Hootalinqua River	320

To	Cassiar Bar	347
"	Little Salmon River	390
"	Five Fingers	451
"	Pelly River (Harpers Post)	510
"	White River	620
"	Stewart River	630
"	Forty Mile Creek	750
"	Circle City	950

OTHER DISTANCES.

To	Sitka, the Capital	160
"	Wrangel	148
"	Seattle	899
"	Cooks Inlet	600
"	San Francisco	1596

ESQUIMAU DOGS.

Much of the transportation about Forty Mile and Circle City is carried on by means of Esquimau Dogs. In the winter time a half-dozen or more are hooked to a sleigh and the driver is able to scud away over the snow at a lively pace with quite a load of freight. In the summer time when the absence of snow renders sleighing impossible, they are used as pack animals, and all kinds of supplies are tied on their backs to be transfered over the rough mountain course to the various camps situated on Birch Creek and other tributaries of the Yukon.

When properly hooked up, a pair of dogs are capable of pulling three or four hundred pounds, and when a dozen or more are attached to one sled they become very efficient for transportation purposes.

The Indians use them exclusively and many mining parties are indebted to their service for a safe passage over the coast range and down the frozen lakes to the Yukon.

During the long winter months they are also used by the mail carriers between Juneau and Circle City, a distance of 1000 miles over a barren frozen country that must be crossed several times during the winter. For this purpose they are invaluable, but on some of these winter trips the weather is so severe that all the dogs are frozen to death and man has difficulty in sustaining life.

From practice and sheer necessity the Esquimau dog has decome accustomed to eating raw fish of which he seems to be very fond. In some sections of the country they can be had at very reasonable prices, but around the interior mining camps good sled dogs are worth fron $100 to $150 each, for transportation purposes.

THE MAILS.

On the establishment of Forty Mile and Circle City on the Yukon the Government found it necessary to extend the mail system to these two camps.

During the summer months when the river is open, this is easy enough done by means of the steamers that make several trips to the main camps and trading posts of the district, but during the long severe winter when the river is frozen and all the country is covered with snow, it becomes necessary to transport the mails across the country from Juneau on snow shoes.

This is a very difficult and dangerous undertaking on account of the distance to be covered and the frequent storms and blizards that sweep over the country during the winter months. Few men, even the hardiest, would care to undertake the trip during severe weather. Nothing but letters are taken by the carriers, and seldome more than one or two thousand at a time.

In the early days the mail did not reach this remote district oftener than once or twice a year, but arrangements have been made lately by which three or four round trips are to be made overland on snow shoes during the winter and as many by steamer during the summer months.

The arrival of the mail at one of these remote camps is an important event of the year, and men, women and children come hurrying from all quarters to hear the news from the outside world.

PRICES ON THE YUKON.

Prices of everything on the Yukon were formerly very high and it was customary for parties to take in enough supplies to last them till they returned, but the competition of the two steamboat lines have cut the prices of things down to such an extent that many parties prefer to buy their supplies at Circle City or Forty Mile.

Ordinarily the cost of provisions and supplies at these two places will be three or four times the amount charged for them in the states. The following will give some idea of the amount paid for staple articles.

Flour per hundred	$8.00
Bacon per pound	.50
Sugar per pound	.33⅓
Lumber per thousand	100.00
Wood per cord	17.00
Gold Dust per ounce	17.00
Esquimau Dogs	100.00 to 150.00

WINTERING ON THE YUKON.

In the early days it was a practice of the miners, and is yet to some extent, to put in a summer's work and get out of the country before the long winter sets in, but of late years many people are wintering in various parts of the country.

About 1000 people will pass the winter of '96 and '97 at Circle City, in order to be on the ground early in the spring for work. A few will operate their claims by thawing the ground and washing out the gold, while others will employ their time in trapping about the country and collecting the valuable furs in which Alaska abounds.

This is one of the greatest fur producing countries in the world. Outside of the enormous number of seals and other valuable skins taken on the coast, the interior abounds in a great variety of valuable pelts, bringing in San Francisco from one to several hundred dollars apiece; and many people profit by collecting these in connection with their prospecting.

COST OF OUTFITS.

The cost of equipping an outfit for making a trip into the interior of Alaska will depend much on the taste, care and good judgement of the purchaser.

Some claim that the trip should not be undertaken with less than $500 per man, but old timers say that with care it can be safely made with half that amount, and many have gone in on almost nothing.

Juneau merchants make a specialty of equipping Yukon miners with outfits costing from $50 to $150, and it is advisable to delay the purchase of provisions at least till Juneau is reached.

Of course, the cost of outfits and the amount to be taken in will depend much on the locality to be visited and the length of time the party expects to be out. If Forty Mile or Circle City is to be visited, then just sufficient provisions may be taken in to

L. of C.

last till one of these camps is reached, where supply houses will furnish you with flour at $6 to $8 per hundred, and other necessities at proportionate prices which are low enough when the grate difficulty of taking supplies in is considered.

On the other hand, if a new section of the country is to be visited enough provisions must be taken in to last till the party returns. It is a good plan for four or five to go together, in which case about 400 pounds per man will make a good outfit, although some take in as much as a ton per man when they expect to be out a couple of years.

At whatever season the trip is made the outfit must be selected and put up with the gratest of care. All perishable goods should be packed in water-tight bags made of skin or of rubber cloth sewed and cemented. This will protect them against any possibility of becoming damaged by snow or rain.

Only the strongest and most substantial foods should be selected, including a good supply of meat, for the game of the country is seldome to be had without going back into the hills after it.

Plenty of arms and amunition, with snow shoes, sleighs, axes, picks, shovels, hand and whip saws should form a part of every outfit. If a boat is not taken it may become necessary to saw up lumber and build one on some of the lakes, and plenty of tar, nails and packing should be taken along for that purpose.

The gratest care must be exercised in the choice of fur and woolen clothing with a water-proof suit, for only the heaviest will be sufficient to keep out the severe cold of the winter and the heavy rains of the summer.

COOKS INLET.

This is a placer mining district on the main land 600 miles west of Sitka. For a number of years the numerous creeks in the district have been prospected with promising results, and late in the fall of '94 rumors of rich deposits brought a horde of miners to the scene.

In the spring the excitement increased and the tide of travel set in for Cook's Inlet. It is an extensive district with many streams and tributaries, hundreds of miles of which have never yet been prospected. Gold is found scattered widely throughout the district in small quantities, showing a certainty of fine deposits somewhere in the vicinity, but as yet only a few rich claims have been located·

CONCERNING PLACERS.

FROM ALASKA NEWS.

All gold, as far as known, was originally deposited in veins imbeded in quartz or other minerals in the mountains, and that now found in placers has been worn out of these veins by the action of the weather, water and glaciers and deposited with the decomposed rocks in its present position in gulches and river beds. The most efficient agents in this work were the glaciers or streams of ice, such as are now at work in the mountains of Alaska, grinding out the precious metals. They were the mills of God, which turned out the gold of most of our placers. They ground slow, but they ground on and on through countless ages, crushing all beneath them and pulverizing the gold bearing rocks.

There is nothing in nature or art so well calculated as glaciers to grind up the rocks and carry the sands, gravels, bolders and gold down into the gulches and deposit them as we find them in our placers.

On the supposition that the gold was brought down by streams of water, it is difficult to explain how so much of it got upon high bars and why the most of it was left on the north and east sides of the gulches; but these are just the places where glaciers would melt most and leave the most of their freight.

With these facts in mind the prospector will find much aid in examining the form of the gulch, to determine where the glacier flowing through it would pile up its freight of ground, where the sun would strike it hottest and melt it most and where it left most of the gravel, for these places would be the richest parts of the placer.

In gulches bordered by high mountains the north and east side would have the most sun and consequently the most gold.

Where the gulch widened out and let in the sun, there the ice river would spread out, melt and leave more or less of its rich load.

Where the gulch opens into a valley is the place where it would finally melt and leave what was left of its precious freight.

CANNING ESTABLISHMENTS.

The Salmon fisheries of Alaska are an immense industry in themselves. More than 619,379 cases of salmon were caught and packed last year and the amount packed this year will be much in excess.

There are twenty-nine canneries in operation, employing about 6000 white men, Chinese and Indians.

The fish supply seems to be inexhaustible. After twelve years of fishing in these waters, and the taking of 288,000,000 pounds, or 144,000 tons of salmon there appears to be more fish this year than ever. In July last at Karlux 100,000 were caught at one haul of the seine.

www.ingramcontent.com/pod-product-compliance
Lightning Source LLC
Chambersburg PA
CBHW022032080426
42733CB00007B/808